27.13

REMARKABLE PEOPLE

Richard Branson

by Steve Goldsworthy

www.av2books.com

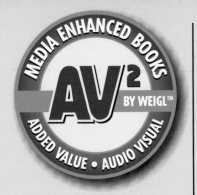

AV² provides enriched content that supplements and complements this book. Weigl's AV² books strive to create inspired learning and engage young minds in a total learning experience.

Your AV² Media Enhanced books come alive with...

Audio
Listen to sections of the book read aloud.

Key Words
Study vocabulary, and complete a matching word activity.

Video
Watch informative video clips.

Quizzes
Test your knowledge.

Embedded Weblinks
Gain additional information for research.

Slide Show
View images and captions, and prepare a presentation.

Try This!
Complete activities and hands-on experiments.

... and much, much more!

Go to www.av2books.com, and enter this book's unique code.

BOOK CODE

L190750

AV² by Weigl brings you media enhanced books that support active learning.

Published by AV² by Weigl
350 5th Avenue, 59th Floor
New York, NY 10118

www.av2books.com   www.weigl.com

Library of Congress Cataloging-in-Publication Data

Goldsworthy, Steve.
 Richard Branson / Steve Goldsworthy.
    p. cm. -- (Remarkable people)
Includes index.
 ISBN 978-1-61690-671-9 (hardcover : alk. paper) -- ISBN 978-1-61690-676-4 (softcover : alk. paper)
1. Branson, Richard. 2. Businessmen--Great Britain--Biography--Juvenile literature. 3. Virgin Group--History--Juvenile literature. I. Title.
HC252.5.B73G65 2011
338'.04092--dc22
[B]
                              2010051145

Printed in the United States of American in North Mankato, Minnesota
1 2 3 4 5 6 7 8 9 0   15 14 13 12 11

WEP37500
052011

Editor: Heather Kissock
Art Director: Terry Paulhus

Photograph Credits
Weigl acknowledges Getty Images and Corbis as the image suppliers for this title.

Every reasonable effort has been made to trace ownership and to obtain permission to reprint copyright material. The publishers would be pleased to have any errors or omissions brought to their attention so that they may be corrected in subsequent printings.

Contents

Who Is Richard Branson?

Richard Branson is a world famous **entrepreneur**, businessman, and **industrialist** from England. He is the founder and owner of Virgin Group Limited, a large conglomerate, or group, of more than 300 companies. Richard and his Virgin Group companies are involved in many businesses, including music, travel, books and publishing, **telecommunications**, and clothing. Virgin is even expanding into space tourism and exploration.

Richard's many amazing accomplishments include writing a best-selling book and hosting his own television show. He holds many world records in **aviation** and exploration, and travels the world inspiring others to live their dreams as he has.

> *"Business opportunities are like buses. There's always another one coming along."*

Growing Up

Richard Charles Nicholas Branson was born on July 18, 1950, in Surrey, England. He was the oldest of four children. His father was a lawyer with a good career and enough money for his children to live comfortably. Their mother, however, taught them to be **self-sufficient**. Richard learned from an early age that he had to work hard if he wanted anything in life.

Richard had the challenge of dealing with **dyslexia** as a young boy. This made school very difficult at times. Growing up, he was an average student, but his dreams were anything but average. While still in school, Richard set up his first business, a school magazine called *Student*. His office was a phone booth in the hall outside one of his classes. He was just 16 years old.

■ Richard Branson attended Stowe School in London, where he excelled at athletics.

Get to Know England

FLOWER
Rose

TREE
Oak

FLAG

London is the capital city of England. It was founded by the Romans almost 2,000 years ago. They named it Londinium.

The London Underground is the oldest subway system in the world. It opened in 1863.

London is the most visited city in the world. More than 300 languages are spoken within its city limits.

French was the official language of England until the 14th century.

Think about it!

Richard Branson moved to London to open his first record shop. Living in a big city has influenced many of Richard Branson's ideas. Think of a large city. Can you see problems with transportation, or air and noise pollution? What solutions could you find to improve the lives of people in your town or city?

Practice Makes Perfect

Even though Richard was not a good student, he attended his classes and worked very hard. His younger brother, Ted, decided to become a lawyer like their father. Richard, however, seemed more interested in getting out in the world and trying new things.

In 1970, at the age of 20, Richard and two friends started a mail-order music service. They believed they could sell records cheaper than regular music stores. The group decided to call their company Virgin. They chose this name because it was their first company, and the word means "first time."

■ Today, Richard's chain of record stores, known as Virgin Megastores, has spread across the globe. Stores can be found in France, Germany, and the Middle East.

One year later, Richard opened the first of several record stores called Virgin Records. In 1972, Richard built a recording studio on Oxford Street. Soon, he was recording musical artists for his record **label**, Virgin Music. Through Richard's hard work, Virgin Music became the sixth largest record label in the world.

■ Simple Minds, a new wave band from Scotland, recorded with Virgin Music. New wave music was developed in the 1970s. It incorporates elements from many other types of music, including punk, electronic, disco, and pop.

Throughout the 1980s, Virgin Music grew larger and expanded into other countries. As a result, Richard traveled quite often. He was often disappointed with his travel experiences. He found his flights uncomfortable. The food was tasteless, and the service was poor. Airlines did not seem to care about their customers. Richard was determined to change this. He decided to create his own airline. On June 22, 1984, Virgin Atlantic had its first flight. Today, the airline carries almost five million passengers around the world each year.

After the success of Virgin Atlantic, Richard set his sights even higher. On September 25, 2004, Virgin Galactic was launched. This company has developed a spaceship, unveiled in 2009, that will eventually take tourists into space.

■ Richard unveiled the plans for his spaceship in New York City, on January 23, 2008.

Thoughts from Richard

One of Richard Branson's greatest talents is his ability to motivate others to realize their dreams and always do their best. Here are things he has said about his success in life.

Richard finds new challenges exciting.

"You never know with these things, when you're trying something new, what can happen. This is all experimental."

Richard has always believed in the importance of family.

"I cannot remember a moment in my life when I have not felt the love of my family."

Richard talks about starting his first business, a school magazine.

"I wanted to be an editor or a journalist. I wasn't really interested in being an entrepreneur, but I soon found I had to become an entrepreneur in order to keep my magazine going."

Richard loves to challenge himself.

"My interest in life comes from setting myself huge, apparently unachievable challenges and trying to rise above them."

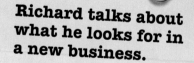

Richard talks about what he looks for in a new business.

"A business has to be involving, it has to be fun, and it has to exercise your creative instincts."

Richard feels strongly that fortunate people like him should help others.

"Ridiculous yachts and private planes and big limousines won't make people enjoy life more... It would be so much better if that money was spent in Africa."

What Is an Entrepreneur?

An entrepreneur is a person who has an idea for a business and is willing to take the risks needed to make it a reality. Almost every industry was started by an entrepreneur of some kind.

An entrepreneur is responsible for raising the money needed to start a new business. Often, that money comes from potential **investors** or banks. Entrepreneurs must convince these investors that the business idea is worthy of investment. This can be difficult. There is no guarantee that the business will succeed.

Richard Branson took a huge risk getting into the airline business. Many of the companies in the industry had been in operation for a long time and were well known. It was difficult for Richard and his Virgin Group to compete with these bigger, established companies.

■ Richard Branson started the Virgin America airline in 2007. It handles flights within North America.

Entrepreneurs 101

P. T. Barnum (1810–1891)

Phineas Taylor Barnum was a pioneer in entertainment. He was a show presenter and businessperson, famous for creating the Barnum & Bailey Circus. Known for his amazing circus and sideshows, he also promoted many acts, including singers, jugglers, and dancers.

Henry Ford (1863–1947)

Henry Ford was an industrialist and the founder of the Ford Motor Company. He created the first **mass-produced** automobile, the Model T Ford, in 1908. He created the **assembly line** technique of mass production. As a result, Ford became one of the richest men in the world at the time.

John D. Rockefeller (1839–1937)

John Davison Rockefeller made millions of dollars from the U.S. demand for kerosene and gasoline. In 1870, he founded a company called Standard Oil. This company grew to dominate the oil industry in the United States. Rockefeller was also a great **philanthropist**. He gave millions to education and medical research.

Oprah Winfrey (1954–)

Oprah Winfrey is a television host, actress, producer, and publisher. She is most famous for her TV talk show, *The Oprah Winfrey Show*, the most successful program of its kind. She has worked hard to give back to her community and has created various foundations for education and health. She is considered one of the most influential women in the world.

The Entrepreneur's Organization

The Entrepreneur's Organization is a global group for entrepreneurs who want to **network** and exchange ideas. The group meets to share their experiences and encourage one another to develop innovative strategies for success. Each member learns new ways to do things, as well as new ways to give back to society.

Influences

Richard's family inspired him in many ways. Both his father and mother taught him the value of hard work. They also encouraged him to be financially independent from an early age. Richard's mother had entrepreneurial skills of her own. When Richard was young, she started her own craft business and sold the items she made to stores in the area.

Richard has found much inspiration from literature. One of his favorite books is Nelson Mandela's autobiography, *Long Walk to Freedom*. Nelson Mandela was a South African **civil rights activist** who, after being imprisoned for 27 years, became South Africa's first black president.

■ Richard Branson is good friends with South African statesman Nelson Mandela.

Richard feels strongly about the environment and the future of the planet. Former U.S. vice-president Al Gore's book *An Inconvenient Truth* is another one of Richard's favorite books. It explores the pollution of Earth and the future of humanity if people do not take action against global warming. The book has inspired Richard to support many environmental causes and to look for alternative forms of fuel and energy for his own businesses.

THE BRANSON FAMILY

Richard married Joan Templeman in 1989 at Necker Island, a small island that Richard owns in the British Virgin Islands. They have two children, Holly, born in 1981, and Sam, born in 1984. Richard gathers strength and inspiration from his family. He is training Holly to take over the company.

■ Richard Branson likes to spend time with his wife and kids. He believes a successful entrepreneur does not spend all of his time at the office.

Overcoming Obstacles

Although Richard Branson has had much success, it has come with many challenges. Throughout his life, Richard has always had people telling him that he could not achieve his goals. Richard, however, has always loved a challenge.

These challenges started early. Richard struggled in school. Along with dyslexia, he was also very nearsighted. This meant he could not see words clearly unless he was very close to them. Even if he could see the words, Richard's dyslexia made it difficult for him to understand what he was reading. His grades suffered as a result. Richard's personality helped him succeed in spite of these conditions. His ambition to succeed and his ability to relate to people allowed Richard to start his own business.

■ By taking on new challenges, Richard has been able to expand his business into a variety of areas. In 2002, he launched his telephone company, Virgin Mobile, in the United States.

Unlike his siblings, Richard did not go to university or college. He did not even complete high school. Even without a formal business education, Richard continued developing businesses and searching for new opportunities. He has always believed that success relies on the courage to try.

■ Over the years, Richard has created an image for his Virgin companies. The Virgin name represents a young, edgy style. Staging Virgin music festivals across the country helps promote this image.

Achievements and Successes

Richard believes strongly that those who have achieved great success must share that success with the world.

In 2005, he created the Branson School of Entrepreneurship at a university in Johannesburg, South Africa. The school helps local South Africans realize their own business dreams and encourages the rest of the world to invest in the growing country.

In 2007, Richard launched the Virgin Earth Challenge, a $25-million award for a company or individual who creates a process to rid the atmosphere of harmful **greenhouse gases**. As well, he has created the Virgin Green Fund to explore **renewable sources** of fuel and energy. Richard also provided funding to an activist group called The Elders. This group seeks peaceful solutions to some of the world's worst conflicts.

■ Former U.S. vice-president Al Gore joined Richard in England to introduce the Virgin Earth Challenge.

In addition to his businesses and charities, Richard has also had time for fun. In 1987, he became the first person to cross the Atlantic Ocean in a hot-air balloon. He also set a hot-air balloon speed record of 245 miles (395 kilometers) per hour on a trip from Japan to Canada's Arctic.

HELPING OTHERS

The Virgin Foundation, or Virgin Unite, is the charitable branch of Richard Branson's Virgin Group. The foundation believes that businesses can work together with governments and communities to create a better world. It provides funding to programs that are working to find positive solutions to social and environmental problems. Founded in 2004, it is run by Virgin Group employees, who donate their time to various charities throughout the world.

Write a Biography

A person's life story can be the subject of a book. This kind of book is called a biography. Biographies describe the lives of remarkable people, such as those who have achieved great success or have done important things to help others. These people may be alive today, or they may have lived many years ago. Reading a biography can help you learn more about a remarkable person.

At school, you might be asked to write a biography. First, decide who you want to write about. You can choose an entrepreneur, such as Richard Branson, or any other person. Then, find out if your library has any books about this person. Learn as much as you can about him or her. Write down the key events in this person's life. What was this person's childhood like? What has he or she accomplished? What are his or her goals? What makes this person special or unusual?

A concept web is a useful research tool. Read the questions in the following concept web. Answer the questions in your notebook. Your answers will help you write a biography.

Richard Branson

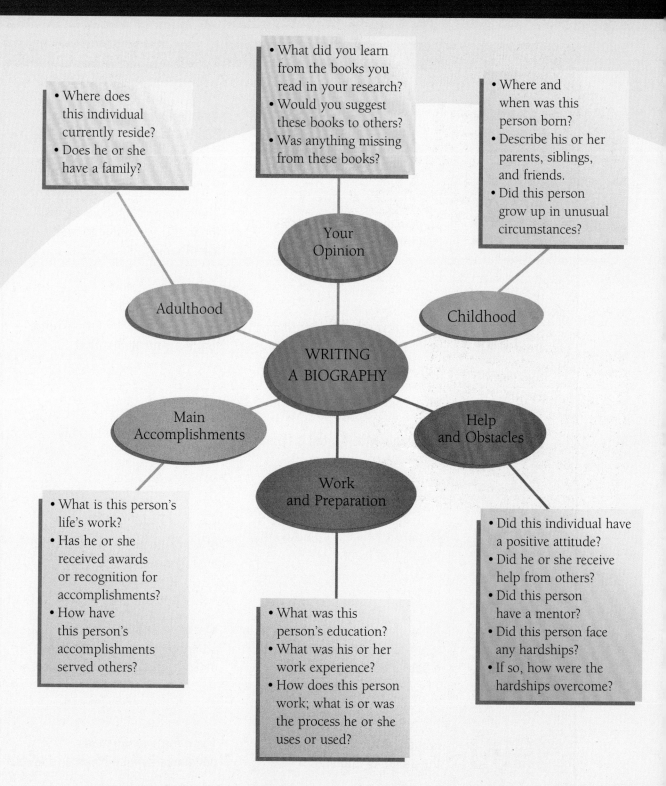

- Where does this individual currently reside?
- Does he or she have a family?

- What did you learn from the books you read in your research?
- Would you suggest these books to others?
- Was anything missing from these books?

- Where and when was this person born?
- Describe his or her parents, siblings, and friends.
- Did this person grow up in unusual circumstances?

Your Opinion

Adulthood

Childhood

WRITING A BIOGRAPHY

Main Accomplishments

Help and Obstacles

Work and Preparation

- What is this person's life's work?
- Has he or she received awards or recognition for accomplishments?
- How have this person's accomplishments served others?

- What was this person's education?
- What was his or her work experience?
- How does this person work; what is or was the process he or she uses or used?

- Did this individual have a positive attitude?
- Did he or she receive help from others?
- Did this person have a mentor?
- Did this person face any hardships?
- If so, how were the hardships overcome?

Timeline

YEAR	RICHARD BRANSON	WORLD EVENTS
1950	Richard Charles Nicholas Branson is born on July 18, in Surrey, England.	**Apartheid** formally begins in South Africa.
1968	*Student* magazine, Richard's first business, is published.	The launch of *Apollo 8* begins the first U.S. mission to orbit the Moon.
1970	Richard creates his record mail order business with two partners.	China becomes the fifth country to put a satellite in orbit.
1973	The Virgin Music label is launched.	The Vietnam War comes to an end.
1984	Richard's airline, Virgin Atlantic, has its first flight.	The first Apple Macintosh, or Mac, computer is introduced on January 24.
1987	Richard becomes the first person to cross the Atlantic Ocean in a hot-air balloon.	Margaret Thatcher wins a third term as prime minister of Great Britain.
1999	Richard is knighted by the queen of England.	The controversial music download service Napster debuts.

Words to Know

Apartheid: a system of racial segregation imposed by the South African government until 1994

assembly line: an arrangement of workers, machines, and equipment in which the product being assembled passes from operation to operation until completed

aviation: the making or flying of an airplane

civil rights activist: a person who supports the rights of others, often through protest

dyslexia: a reading and learning disorder

entrepreneur: a person who takes on the risk and responsibility of a new idea, business, or product

greenhouse gases: gases in the atmosphere that trap the Sun's energy and contribute to rising temperatures

industrialist: a person who owns a manufacturing company

investors: people who give money to a company in order to make a profit

label: a brand used to market music

mass-produced: created in large quantities

network: to meet others, usually in a similar industry, for the purpose of exchanging ideas

philanthropist: a person, usually very wealthy, who helps others, often through charity

renewable sources: items that can be used over and over again

self-sufficient: able to rely on yourself

telecommunications: the transmission of information over long distances, usually using electronics and other technologies

Index

Log on to www.av2books.com

AV² by Weigl brings you media enhanced books that support active learning. Go to www.av2books.com, and enter the special code found on page 2 of this book. You will gain access to enriched and enhanced content that supplements and complements this book. Content includes video, audio, web links, quizzes, a slide show, and activities.

Audio
Listen to sections of the book read aloud.

Video
Watch informative video clips.

Embedded Weblinks
Gain additional information for research.

Try This!
Complete activities and hands-on experiments.

WHAT'S ONLINE?

Try This!	Embedded Weblinks	Video	EXTRA FEATURES
Complete an activity about your childhood.	Learn more about Richard Branson's life.	Watch a video about Richard Branson.	**Audio** Listen to sections of the book read aloud.
Try this activity about key events.	Learn more about Richard Branson's achievements.	Check out another video about Richard Branson.	**Key Words** Study vocabulary, and complete a matching word activity.
Complete an activity about overcoming obstacles.	Check out this site about Richard Branson.		**Slide Show** View images and captions, and prepare a presentation.
Write a biography.			**Quizzes** Test your knowledge.
Try this timeline activity.			

AV² was built to bridge the gap between print and digital. We encourage you to tell us what you like and what you want to see in the future.

Sign up to be an AV² Ambassador at www.av2books.com/ambassador.